lampwork

Lampwork: Decorative Projects To Light Up The

London: Southwater, 1998   1842153749

lampwork

Decorative projects to light up the home

Isabel Stanley
Photography by Lizzie Orme

southwater

This edition is published by Southwater

Southwater is an imprint of
Anness Publishing Limited
Hermes House
88–89 Blackfriars Road
London SE1 8HA
tel. 020 7401 2077
fax 020 7633 9499

Distributed in the USA by
Anness Publishing Inc.
27 West 20th Street
Suite 504
New York
NY 10011
fax 212 807 6813

Distributed in the UK by
The Manning Partnership
251–253 London Road East
Batheaston
Bath BA1 7RL
tel. 01225 852 727
fax 01225 852 852

Distributed in Australia by
Sandstone Publishing
Unit 1
360 Norton Street
Leichhardt
New South Wales 2040
tel. 02 9560 7888
fax 02 9560 7488

1 3 5 7 9 10 8 6 4 2

Publisher: Joanna Lorenz
Senior Editor: Catherine Barry
Designer: Julie Francis
Illustrator: Lucinda Ganderton
Photographer: Lizzie Orme
Step Photography: Steven Pam
Stylist: Jo Rigg

Care must be taken with lampshades. All electrical appliances can be dangerous.

MEASUREMENTS
Both imperial and metric measurements have been given in the text.
Where conversions produce an awkward number, these have been rounded for convenience,
but will produce an accurate result if one system is used throughout.

Previously published as *Inspirations: Lampshades*

CONTENTS

INTRODUCTION

WHEN I WAS A CHILD I remember my mother making a matching set of 12 beautifully-crafted, chiffon, pleated lampshades. She began with enthusiasm, carefully folding, pressing and stitching, finishing the first few with ease. By the fourth shade her enthusiasm was starting to flag. The amount of time and effort she spent working on these matching shades discouraged me for years from making my own lampshades.

Now I have a home of my own, I find that one of the most tricky things about furnishing a room is getting the lighting right and creating the right mood. If you are lucky you may find a perfect pendant shade in a store, but what about matching wall lights or co-ordinated standard lamps? If you want a personal, harmonious feel to your room, it is far easier (and less expensive) to follow in my mother's footsteps and make your own. Nowadays modern, easy-to-use equipment and materials will cut down the time and amount of effort you will need to spend on making your own shades and there are hundreds of stylish ideas to choose from to suit your taste and pocket.

This book has given me lots of ideas which are surprisingly simple to make. You can start with a simple shade and embellish it with a country-style frill, colourful raffia or sophisticated beads, or you can create a new shade from scratch, using the templates and techniques provided. You can use paint, fabric, ribbons, paper, beads...the possibilities are endless. You don't have to worry about finding a base to match either, as we give ideas for customizing store-bought bases to suit the shades. With full step-by-step instructions and comprehensive materials, equipment and techniques sections, this book will ensure impressive results with the minimum of effort.

So don't bother searching for the perfect shade any longer. Simply look through this book and you will find the styles to suit your needs and skills.

Deborah Barker

BEADED FRINGE LAMPSHADE

Round and teardrop-shaped glass beads in harmonizing tones of blue, green and purple make a delicate, sparkling fringe to transform a plain ready-made shade. This traditional trimming looks perfectly at home on a modern lamp.

YOU WILL NEED
tape measure
needle
ready-made lampshade
beading needle
matching sewing thread
2 mm/¹⁄₁₂ in purple faceted round crystal beads
4 mm/¹⁄₆ in purple faceted round crystal beads
2 mm/¹⁄₁₂ in green faceted round crystal beads
tiny purple glass beads
8 mm/⅜ in blue teardrop crystal beads
decorative ribbon
scissors
all-purpose glue

1 Using a tape measure and an ordinary needle, punch holes 8 mm/⅜ in apart and 5 mm/¼ in from the lower edge of the shade.

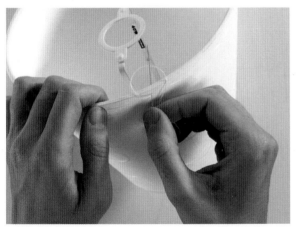

2 Thread a beading needle, double up the thread and knot the ends. Insert the needle through the first hole, working from the inside of the shade. Make a loop of thread around your finger and pass the needle back through the first hole. Bring the needle down to the lower edge of the shade, pass it through the loop and draw the thread up tight.

3 Arrange the beads in small bowls, sorted according to type and colour. Line the bowls up in the order in which you assemble the fringe. Thread a small purple crystal bead on to the hanging thread, followed by a larger purple one. Then thread on one round green bead and three tiny purple glass beads. Thread on a blue teardrop crystal bead.

4 Thread on three more tiny purple beads, then pass the needle back through the small green, large purple and small purple beads.

5 Take the thread back through the first hole to complete the first string of beads, then insert the needle in the second hole.

6 Make a loop on the inside of the shade and make a second beaded string. Repeat steps 2–5, creating a beaded fringe all around the lower edge of the shade where you have made holes. Make sure that the beads are added in the same order on each string for consistency.

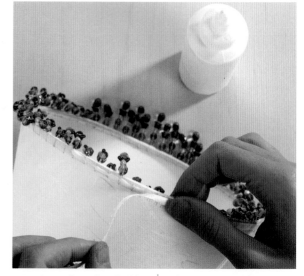

7 Cut a length of ribbon to fit around the lower edge of the shade, plus 2.5 cm/1 in turning allowance. Apply a line of glue around the shade and press the ribbon in place, concealing all the threads. Turn the ribbon end under by 1.5 cm/⅝ in and lap it (press down) over the other end.

RUFFLE TRIMMED SHADE

The ruffled trimming around this shade has a fresh summery look, like the curly leaves of young lettuces or parsley – the rich textural effect is achieved by pinking the edges and using two subtly different shades of green cotton.

YOU WILL NEED
ruler
tailor's chalk
scissors
plain cotton fabric in two shades of lime green,
each 100 x 50 cm/39 x 20 in
pinking shears
needle
matching thread
pins
ready-made Oriental shade with reversible gimbal, top ring
12 cm/4 ¾ in diameter, bottom ring 36 cm/14 in diameter
PVA (white) glue

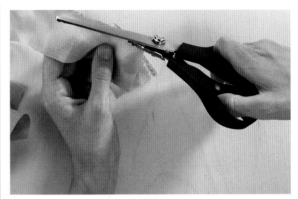

1 Mark and cut out six 100 x 5 cm/39 x 2 in strips of each fabric. Carefully trim the edges with pinking shears. Join three strips by the short edges, using running stitch, to make two long strips of each colour. Assemble the strips on top of each other, alternating the colours, and pin together. For the top ring, cut three 36 x 4 cm/14 x 1¾ in strips of each colour and join to make two long strips. Pin together.

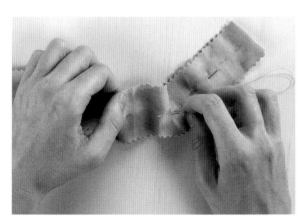

2 Thread a needle, double up the thread and knot the ends. Sew a line of running stitch along the middle of each set of strips, through all thicknesses.

3 Holding an end firmly with one hand, draw up all the threads with the other hand, pulling tightly to obtain a rucked, frilled effect.

4 Using your fingers, or a pin if necessary, loosen the stitches and even out the gathers of the lower frill, adjusting the length of the frilled strip until it fits around the bottom edge of the lampshade.

5 Apply a line of glue around the bottom edge of the shade and press the centre line of the frill. Where the ends meet, turn one end under, lap it over the other and glue. Repeat with the upper frill.

6 Pinch the edges of the uppermost strips of each frill together at even intervals and secure with glue. Leave to dry.

GREEN GLASS BEADED SHADE

For this opulent treatment, thousands of small green glass beads are threaded on to gold wire and woven around a golden frame. The wooden lampbase has been gilded too, so that the whole lamp will glitter and glow when it is turned on.

YOU WILL NEED
protective face mask
gold spray paint
straight empire lampshade frame with bulb clip, top diameter
7.5 cm/3 in, bottom diameter 12 cm/4¾ in, height 11 cm/4¼ in
0.6 mm/¹⁄₄₀ in gold-plated jewellery wire
jewellery pliers and cutters
tiny green glass beads (sold on the string)
fine brass wire
wooden lamp base
fine-grade sandpaper
spray adhesive
Dutch gold leaf
paintbrush or teaspoon
spray varnish

1 If necessary, protect your work surface with newspaper, brown paper or a sheet of plastic. Wearing a protective face mask, spray the empire-shaped lampshade frame with gold spray paint and leave to dry. Apply another coat if necessary. Again, leave to dry thoroughly.

2 Make a small loop at one end of a 1 m/1 yd length of gold-plated jewellery wire. You can use ordinary wire if you wish. Transfer the ready-strung green beads on to the wire by passing the straight end of the wire through the beads alongside the string, then removing the string. Thread beads along almost the entire length of the wire, leaving about 2.5cm/1 in spare at the end.

14

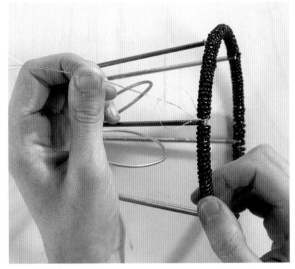

3 Spiral the free end of the wire around the bottom ring of the shade and secure it with a small knot. Wind the beaded wire all around the bottom ring, finishing off with another small knot. Wrap the top ring in the same way.

4 For each upright strut, cut a piece of fine brass wire with the pliers about four times the height of the shade. Loop the middle of each wire around the bottom of a strut, pass the ends through the loop and pull tight.

5 Cut another length of gold-plated wire 3 m/10 ft long and thread with beads as before. Spiral the free end of the wire around the base of an upright strut. Wrap the beaded wire around the frame, weaving the finer wires over the beaded wire and around the struts, to secure the beads to the frame.

6 When you reach the top of the frame, finish off by tying a firm, small knot in each fine wire around the top ring. Tie off the beaded wire around the top of an upright strut. Neaten the top edges, bending any stray wires inwards and under to conceal them from view.

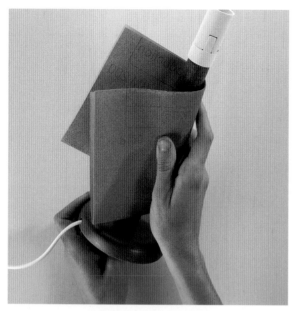

7 To decorate the base, rub down the wood to remove any varnish, using fine-grade sandpaper.

8 Wearing a protective mask, coat the base with spray adhesive and leave until it feels tacky.

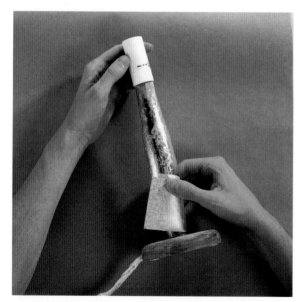

9 Wrap the Dutch gold leaf face down around the lamp base. Rub over the backing paper with a dry paintbrush or the back of a teaspoon, then peel away the backing. Cut more pieces to size to cover the rest of the base in the same manner.

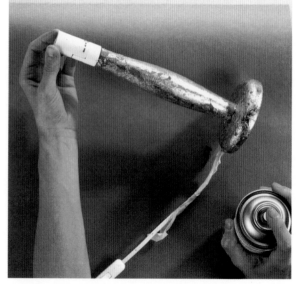

10 Lightly rub the base to remove any loose pieces of gold leaf. Seal the gold leaf with a coat of spray varnish, wearing a protective mask. Leave to dry thoroughly. Attach the shade to the base, and fit with a low-wattage bulb.

RUSTIC GINGHAM

This country-style shade has lots of simple charm yet isn't too frilly or frivolous, thanks to the strong contrasting colours of the natural fabrics and the neatly tailored pleats of the "skirt".

YOU WILL NEED
paper
pencil
empire lampshade frame with reversible gimbal, top diameter 10 cm/4 in, bottom diameter 20 cm/8 in, height 16 cm/6¼ in
tailor's chalk
scissors
self-adhesive lampshade backing material
0.5 m/½ yd red cotton drill (twill)
PVA (white) glue
binding tape
clothes pegs (pins)
green medium-weight gingham, 80 x 22 cm/32 x 8¾ in
pins
needle
matching thread
iron
red ric-rac braid
red acrylic paint
paintbrush
wooden lamp base

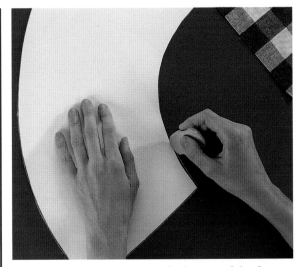

1 Make a paper pattern to fit the size of the frame you have chosen (see Techniques). Cut a piece of self-adhesive backing material to the size of the paper pattern. Place the pattern on the red fabric and cut out on the bias, adding a 1.5 cm/⅝ in turning allowance all around.

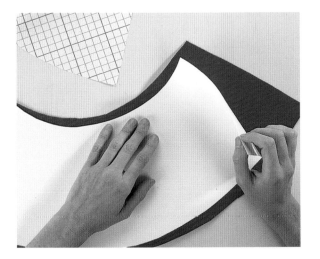

2 Lay the red cotton drill (twill) fabric face down on your work surface and position the backing material centrally. Smooth out the fabric from the middle outwards to eliminate any creases. Turn in and using PVA (white) glue, stick down the fabric allowance (see Techniques). Then wrap the lampshade frame with binding tape. Apply lines of PVA (white) glue to the outside of the rings and the upright struts of the frame. Wrap the backed fabric around the frame. Apply a line of PVA (white) glue to the underside of the overlap and stick to the opposite edge of the shade. Use two clothes pegs (pins) to hold the edges together. Leave until the glue is completely dry.

3 Turn and pin a 1.5 cm/⅝ in hem along both long edges of the gingham and slip-stitch the hem. Turn under 1 cm/½ in along each short edge and press.

4 Along the top edge, at 2cm/¾ in intervals, press in pleats 2 cm/¾ in wide, pin and tack (baste). Slip-stitch the short edges together.

5 Run a line of glue around the shade, 2 cm/¾ in below the top edge. Wrap the gingham skirt around the shade, 1 cm/½ in below the top edge. Use clothes pegs (pins) to hold the skirt in place while the glue dries. Cut a piece of ric-rac braid to fit around the pleats, plus 2 cm/¾ in overlap. Glue the braid into position, about 5 mm/¼ in from the top edge of the gingham. Turn under the end of the ric-rac and glue it over the other raw end.

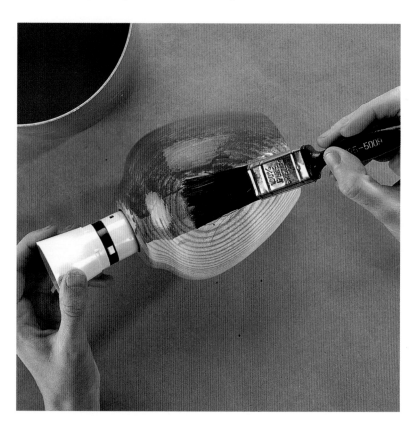

6 For the base, thin some red acrylic paint with water or white spirit and paint a light wash over the plain wooden lamp base, so that the grain is still visible. Leave to dry completely. Apply another coat if you require a deeper colour. When dry, attach the shade to the base. Spray the shade with flame retarder (see Techniques) if you are using a high-wattage bulb, otherwise use a low-wattage bulb.

APPLIQUÉD FLOWERS AND LEAVES

Perfect for a romantically decorated bedroom, this delicate silk lampshade is scattered with tiny flowers. The leaves, cut from the same fabric as the shade, are stitched on to the silk before backing. Glossy satin binding completes the design.

YOU WILL NEED
paper
pencil
straight empire lampshade frame
with reversible gimbal, top diameter
10 cm/4 in, bottom diameter 20 cm/8 in,
height 16 cm/6¼ in
scissors
self-adhesive lampshade backing
material
0.5 m/½ yd white silk dupion
iron
fusible bonding web
card for template
embroidery scissors
sewing machine
matching thread
PVA (white) glue
artificial flowers
satin bias binding (tape)
glue gun
clothes pegs (pins)
needle
wooden lamp base
fine-grade sandpaper
white acrylic paint
paintbrush

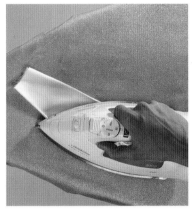

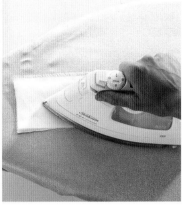

1 Make a paper pattern to fit the frame you have chosen (see Techniques). Cut a piece of self-adhesive backing material to the size of the paper pattern. Carefully cut out the silk fabric, placing the pattern on the bias and adding a 1.5 cm/⅝ in turning allowance all round. Fold the fabric in half three times, and press in the folds with an iron to mark eight sections.

2 Cut a piece of fusible bonding web 15 x 7.5 cm/ 6 x 3 in and a piece of white silk to the same size. Lay the bonding web on a flat surface, adhesive side down on the wrong side of the silk and fuse in place with an iron. Be careful to follow the manufacturer's instructions on the bonding web for the temperature setting on your iron or you may scorch the silk.

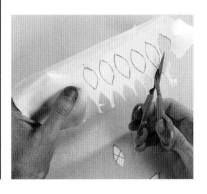

3 Copy the leaf design from the back of the book and make a template from stiff, thick card. Draw around the template on to the backing paper 16 times. Cut out the leaf shapes carefully, using a pair of small, sharp embroidery scissors.

▶

4 Open out the silk. Peel away the backing paper from each leaf shape and arrange a pair of leaves on either side of each fold line in the silk, 5 cm/2 in from the fabric edge, alternately at the top and bottom of the shade or according to your own design. Fuse in place with an iron. Again, take care to set the iron to the correct temperature as recommended by the manufacturer of the backing fabric.

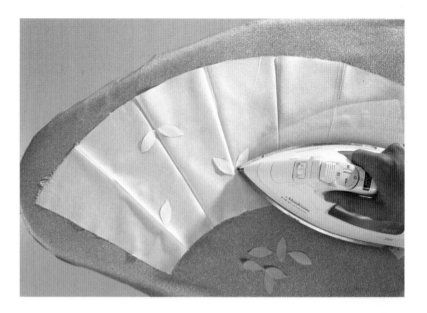

6 Lay the appliquéd fabric face down and position the large piece of backing material in the centre. Smooth out the fabric from the middle outwards. Turn in and glue the fabric allowance (see Techniques). Snip the artificial flowers from their stems. Apply a small blob of PVA (white) glue to each flower and stick a neat row along the top edge of the shade. Stick a flower in the middle of each pair of leaves.

5 Setting your sewing machine to zig-zag mode, work a narrow zig-zag stitch around each shape using matching thread.

7 Cut a piece of satin bias binding (tape) the length of the bottom edge of the silk plus 2 cm/¾ in. Using the glue gun, apply a line of glue or PVA (white) glue to the bottom edge of the shade and press one long edge of the binding to the edge of the silk. Turn the other long edge to the inside and glue to the shade in the same way. Leave to dry completely before proceeding to the next step.

8 Apply a line of glue along the underside of one side edge, roll the shade into a cone and lap (press) the glued edge over the opposite edge. Use two clothes pegs (pins) to hold the edge firmly together until the glue is dry. Check that the cover fits the frame. Slip-stitch the folded edges. Apply lines of glue around the outside edges of the frame and insert the frame into the cover.

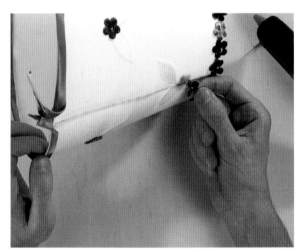

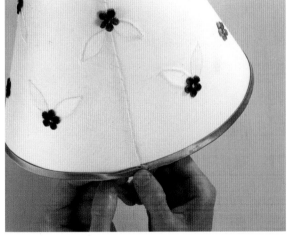

9 Stick the rest of the artificial flowers along the top edge to obsure the seam of the shade, and between the final pair of leaves. Leave to dry completely.

10 Where the ends of the bias binding meet, turn under 1 cm/½ in of one raw end and stick it down with a blob of glue so that it overlaps the other raw end. Use two clothes pegs to hold the ends firmly until the glue is dry. ▶

11 Rub down the wooden lamp base with fine-grade sandpaper to remove the varnish or any other finish.

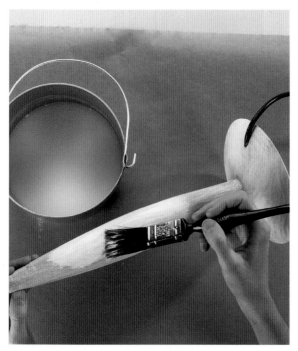

12 Apply a thin coat of white acrylic paint, leave to dry thoroughly, then rub down again to create a distressed effect. Spray the shade with flame retarder if necessary and dry completely. Attach the base to the shade and use a low-wattage bulb for a romantic bedside glow.

POMPOM LAMPSHADE

These oversized multicoloured pompoms are a quirky reinterpretation of bobble lampshade fringing. The rest of the decoration is quick to do, using oil pastels to stripe a plain lampshade, and ceramic paints for the matching base.

YOU WILL NEED
pencil
white ready-made Oriental lampshade
oil pastels
pompom-making kit or card
pair of compasses (compass)
scissors
cotton yarn, in five contrasting shades
selection of 5 mm/¼ in wide ribbons
large needle
thimble (optional)
enamel or ceramic paints
paintbrush
white ceramic lamp base

1 Using a pencil, mark lines from the top edge of the shade to the bottom, spreading them out evenly around the bottom circumference.

2 Draw thick lines over the pencil marks using different shades of oil pastel.

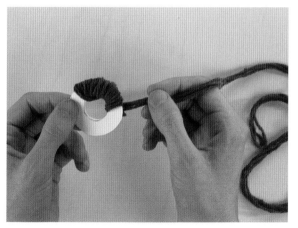

3 Make the pompoms by drawing two 6.5 cm/2½ in diameter circles on a piece of card. Draw a 2.5 cm/1 in diameter circle inside each one. Cut around the outer and inner circles. Holding the two card circles together, wrap the cotton yarn around them until the central hole is full.

4 Place one blade of the scissors between the two pieces of card and cut the yarn. Tie a length of ribbon or yarn around the centre, between the two cards (cardboard pieces). Pull one side of the pompom through the holes to remove the cards and fluff out the yarn. Make ten pompoms, using different colours.

5 Using a large needle, punch ten evenly spaced holes around the bottom edge of the shade. You may like to wear a thimble for this to protect your fingers. Thread one end of the ribbon or yarn tied around each pompom through a hole from the outside and tie the two ends in a tight knot.

6 Paint horizontal stripes of colour around the lamp base using enamel or ceramic paints. Leave to dry before fixing the shade to the base.

WRAPPED SILK PENDANT

Richly coloured raw silk and gold tassels make a sumptuous pendant lampshade. Cut on the bias, the silk drapes beautifully around the frame and its natural crispness is further enhanced by painting it with a coat of fabric stiffener.

YOU WILL NEED
70 cm/¾ yd raw silk fabric, 120 cm/48 in wide
iron
tailor's chalk
ruler
scissors
pins
sewing machine
matching thread
fabric stiffener
jar
old paintbrush
square lampshade frame with pendant fitting,
top 18 cm/7 in across, bottom 10 cm/4 in across,
height 40 cm/16 in
PVA (white) glue
4 ready-made tassels
needle

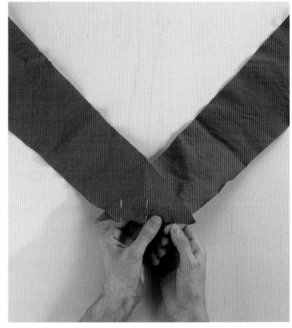

1 Bias strips of brightly-coloured silk are used to wrap the frame. Starting with a rectangular piece of fabric cut on the straight grain, fold one top corner down to the bottom edge to form a diagonal fold. Press, using an iron on a low setting and open out. Mark diagonal lines parallel to the fold across the fabric 10 cm/4 in apart and cut out. Join the strips together by placing the ends right sides together to form a right angle. Pin and stitch 1.5 cm/⅝ in from the raw edges. Make a separate bias strip 4 cm/1½ in wide to cover the bottom of the frame.

2 Join the wide and narrow pieces of silk together to form two continuous strips. Carefully trim the seam allowances without fraying the fabric and press open using a cool iron.

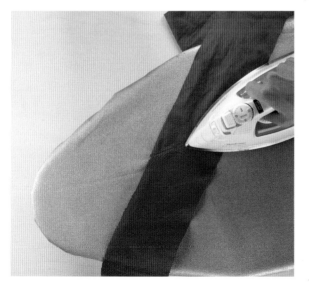

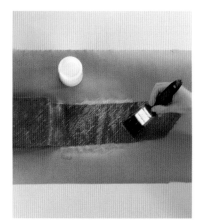

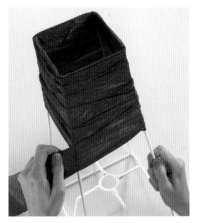

3 Pour a small quantity of fabric stiffener into a clean jar. Lay the strips of silk out, right sides down and, using an old paintbrush, paint them with a coat of stiffener. Apply two coats if necessary. Leave to dry.

4 To cover the square frame, wrap the bottom end of the frame with the narrow strip of stiffened silk, stretching the fabric taut. Make sure that you cover the frame completely and make a neat join where the ends meet.

5 Using the wider strip of stiffened silk, press one end to the bottom of the frame and pin. Wrap the strip around the frame, stretching the fabric taut. Tuck the raw edges into the folds and ruche the fabric as you work.

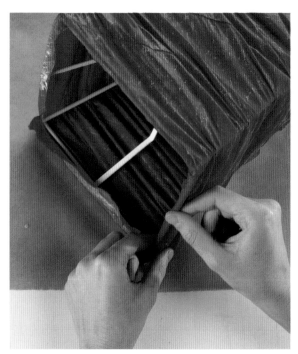

6 At the top of the frame, fold the raw edges over the frame to the inside and glue into position.

7 Stitch a tassel to each corner of the narrow bottom end of the frame.

PLEATED PAPER LAMPSHADE

Use creamy handmade paper and tissue, with their subtle variations of texture, to make this understated pendant. Slivers of gold leaf, protected under the upper layer of tissue paper, glint almost imperceptibly from between the pleats.

YOU WILL NEED
conical lampshade frame, top diameter 7.5 cm/3 in, bottom diameter 30 cm/12 in, height 14 cm/5½ in
tape measure
A1 (594 x 841 mm/23⅜ x 33⅛ in) sheet handmade paper
scissors
pencil
metal ruler
spray adhesive and face mask
Dutch gold leaf
teaspoon
A1 (594 x 841 mm/23⅜ x 33⅛ in) sheet handmade tissue paper
thick card for template
hole punch
PVA (white) glue
40 cm/16 in ribbon

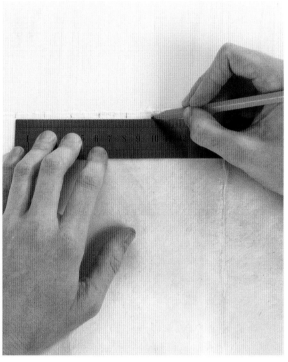

1 Measure the circumference of the bottom edge of the lampshade frame with a tape measure and multiply this measurement by two. Add a 2 cm/¾ in overlap. Measure the side of the frame and add 5 cm/2 in. Cut a rectangle from the paper to these dimensions. If you are using smaller sheets of paper, first join the sheets with a 2 cm/¾ in overlap. On the wrong side of the paper at the top and bottom, mark points 2 cm/¾ in apart using a pencil.

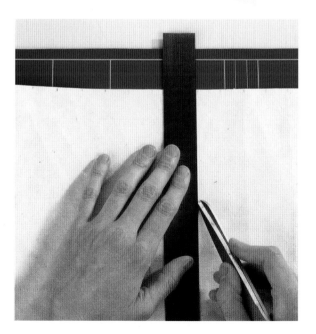

2 To make the pleats, join up the marks with a metal ruler and score creases down the length of the paper with the blunt tip of a scissor blade. Fold in the pleats.

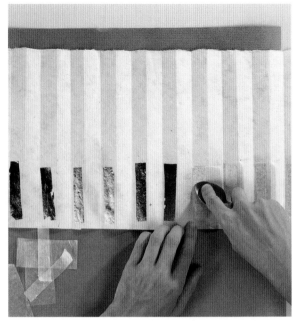

3 Apply spray adhesive along the lower part of the folded paper, wearing a face mask. Cut strips of Dutch gold leaf 5 x 1 cm/2 x ½ in, and place them face down along the bottom edge between the folds.

4 Rub over the backing paper thoroughly with the back of a teaspoon and remove the paper. Cut a piece of tissue paper to the same size as the handmade paper in step 1.

5 Spray a coat of adhesive over the handmade paper and stick the tissue paper in place.

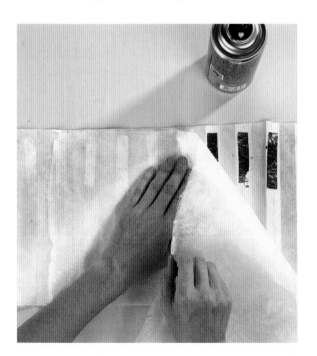

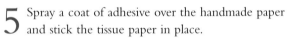

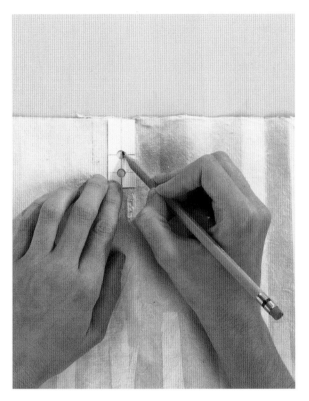

6 Make a template to mark the positions of the two rows of holes, cutting a piece of thick card 5 x 2 cm/2 x ¾ in and drawing a line down the centre. Using a hole punch, punch holes on the central line, 1.5 cm/⅝ in and 3 cm/1¼ in from the top edge.

7 Align the template with the top edge of each folded pleat and mark the holes. Use the hole punch to make a pair of holes on the sides of each pleat at the pencil marks.

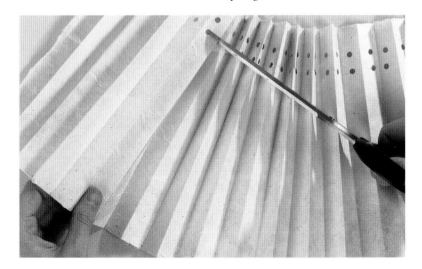

8 Using a pair of scissors, cut across to the lower row of holes from the inside of each pleat, except the end ones. ▶

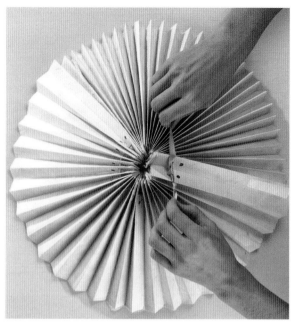

9 To join the end pleats, spread a line of PVA (white) glue along one side edge and press the other end in place. Mark the positions of the holes and punch them with a hole punch as before.

10 Thread the ribbon through the upper row of holes. Draw up the ribbon tightly, tie a knot at the top and trim the ends. Leave the ends of the ribbon to hang down over the paper join.

11 Fit the lower row of holes over the upper ring of the lampshade frame. Spread out the pleats evenly. Spray with flame retarder if necessary. Fix shade to the ceiling attachment over a medium-wattage bulb.

CHUNKY BEADED DRUM

Use large glass beads in an assortment of colours and shapes, interspersed with smaller gold ones, for a jewel-encrusted, sparkling shade. Space the larger beads at random along the wires so that each one is framed by the small beads.

YOU WILL NEED
drum-shaped lampshade frame with reversible gimbal, top diameter 20 cm/8 in, bottom diameter 25 cm/10 in, height 25 cm/10 in
gold spray paint and face mask
fine brass wire
jewellery pliers and cutters
0.6 mm/¹⁄₄₀ in gold-plated jewellery wire
small flat round gold crystal beads
selection of chunky glass beads
ceramic lamp base
brown acrylic paint
dish
kitchen sponge
cloth (clean cotton rag)
picture framer's wax gilt

1 Spray the frame with gold paint. Wear a face mask and work in a well-ventilated area.

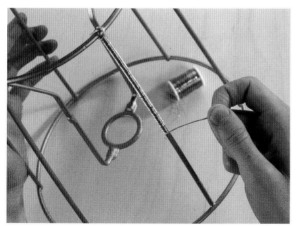

2 For each upright strut, cut a piece of brass wire approximately 3 m/10 ft long. When the frame is dry, fold the wire in half and in half again, loop it over the top ring and wind the strands down each strut. Finish at the base of the strut with a small knot.

3 Cut a piece of the thicker jewellery wire approximately 70 cm/28 in long and spiral one end about five times around the top ring next to a strut. Thread enough beads on to the wire to fit between the top and bottom rings, including a few large ones.

4 Spiral the long end around the bottom ring about five times and pull up tightly. Thread on the same number of beads, then spiral the long end around the top ring. Snip the end with the cutters. Continue back and forth in this way all round the shade.

5 Cut a piece of the fine wire approximately 3 m/10 ft long, fold in half and in half again. Loop the wire around an upright strut and spiral the strands closely around the bottom ring, finishing with a small knot. Wrap the top ring in the same way.

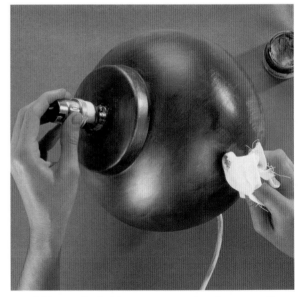

6 To decorate the base, squeeze some brown acrylic paint into a dish, dab a sponge in the paint and wipe it over the base in an uneven criss-cross manner, avoiding the brass fitting. Leave to dry completely.

7 Using a cloth (clean cotton rag), wipe wax gilt over the paint, rubbing harder in some areas to give an uneven finish. Leave to dry completely before attaching the shade.

RAFFIA CROSS-STITCH SHADE

Big, bold cross stitches and an unruly fringe make good use of dyed raffia in bright, paintbox colours to create a design with humour and panache. Paint a fifties-style lamp base in equally gaudy colours to set off this shade with aplomb.

YOU WILL NEED
tapestry needle
selection of dyed raffia
ready-made straight empire lampshade
scissors
1 cm/½ in wide cotton tape
sewing machine
matching thread
strong, clear (epoxy) glue
velvet ribbon
ric-rac braid
wooden lamp base
acrylic paints in pink and lavender
paintbrush
wax furniture polish
cloth (clean cotton rag) or sponge
fine-grade sandpaper

1 Thread a tapestry needle with a strand of raffia 60 cm/24 in long and double up the raffia. Push the needle through the shade just above the rim and pull half the length of the raffia through. Tie the ends of the raffia in a double knot just underneath the rim. Trim the ends with scissors to release the needle. Repeat at 2 cm/¾ in intervals all round the shade.

2 Cut a length of tape to fit the circumference of the top ring of the shade. Cut pieces of raffia at least 3 cm/1¼ in long. Lay the tape on the bed of a sewing machine and arrange the raffia pieces along the tape. Using matching thread, stitch the raffia to the tape. Trim the fringe to a 2 cm/¾ in length.

3 Using strong (epoxy) glue, stick the fringe around the top edge of the shade. Cut a piece of ribbon and a piece of ric-rac braid to fit the top circumference, plus 2 cm/¾ in turning allowance. Apply a line of glue around the centre of the fringe and press the ribbon in position. Where the raw ends meet, turn under 1 cm/½ in of one end, lap it over the opposite end and glue in place. Glue the ric-rac in the centre of the ribbon, neatening the ends as before.

4 Using a tapestry needle and brightly-coloured selection of raffia lengths, stitch randomly-positioned cross-wise stitches all over the shade.

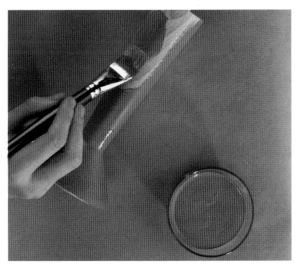

5 Apply two coats of the base colour paint to the lamp base and allow to dry between applications.

6 When dry, rub a layer of wax furniture polish over the paint using a cloth (clean cotton rag). ▶

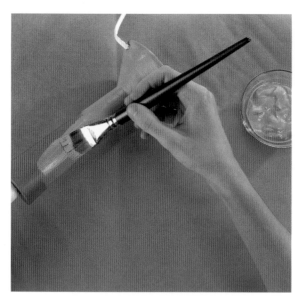

7 Paint on one coat of the final colour for the lamp base and leave to dry thoroughly.

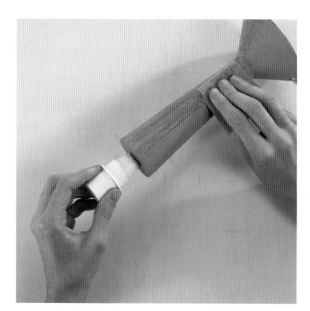

8 Rub down the paint with fine-grade sandpaper to create a distressed effect and allow some of the base colour to show through. Remove any dust with a damp cloth (rag) or sponge and leave to dry. If necessary, spray the shade with flame retarder before attaching to the base. Use a low-wattage bulb.

PAPER STAR

This fabulous three-dimensional star will light your room with a soft and flattering golden glow. Choose thick, creamy handmade paper with an interesting texture and add tiny cut-out stars as a finishing touch.

YOU WILL NEED
card for template
scissors
craft knife
pencil
3 x A1 (594 x 841 mm/23⅜ x 33⅛ in) sheets handmade paper
metal ruler
white tissue paper
PVA (white) glue
hole punch
30 cm/12 in gold cord
2 small buttons
pendant light fitting

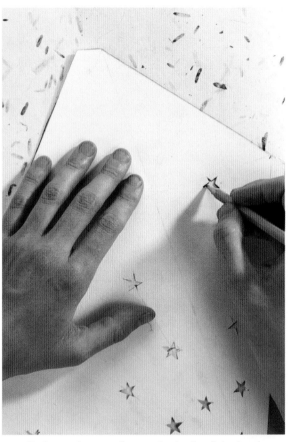

1 Scale up the template at the back of the book to your required size, copy it on to card and cut it out. Carefully cut out the small star shapes using a sharp craft knife. Using a pencil, draw around the template five times onto the handmade paper and cut out with scissors.

2 Score along the fold lines of each section on the template using the blunt side of the craft knife and a metal ruler. Cut between tabs C to separate.

3 Cut out a piece of tissue paper to line each section. Apply glue to the back of the handmade paper and stick the tissue paper down on to it.

4 Take the first section and apply a line of glue to the front of tab A and stick it to the underside of edge B. Repeat for the other four sections.

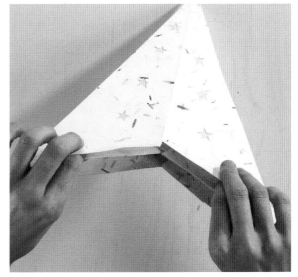

5 To assemble the star, apply a small blob of PVA (white) glue to the front of tabs C of one section and press them inside edges D of the next section. Apply a line of glue to the back of tabs C of the last section and fold them under. Leave the glue to dry.

6 Mark a small cross 2 cm/¾ in from the edges near the centre fold on each side of the opening. Cut two 2 cm/¾ in squares of handmade paper and glue to the inside under each cross.

7 Using a hole punch, make a single hole at each cross mark on the shade. These will form the eyelets used to suspend the shade from the pendant light fitting.

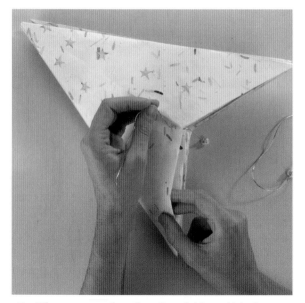

8 Then cut two lengths of cord 15 cm/6 in long and tie a small button to one end of each length. Thread each cord through one of the holes from the insides – the buttons should act as anchors.

9 Insert the pendant light fitting into the shade through the top and open out the star. Tie the two cords together and around the flex. Spray with flame retarder if necessary. Use a low-wattage bulb.

PURPLE CORDED LAMPSHADE

This sophisticated, one-colour design concentrates on surface texture, using slubby (textured) raw silk dupion as the background for elegant curlicues of couched silk cord which neatly echo the curly shapes of the wrought iron base.

YOU WILL NEED
paper
pencil
straight empire lampshade frame with reversible gimbal, top diameter 10 cm/4 in, bottom diameter 20 cm/8 in, height 16 cm/6 ¼ in
scissors
self-adhesive lampshade backing material
0.5 m/½ yd purple silk dupion
tailor's chalk
purple cording
needle
matching thread
PVA (white) glue
binding tape
clothes pegs (pins)
wrought iron lamp base

1 Make a paper pattern to fit the lampshade frame you have chosen (see Techniques). Cut a piece of self-adhesive backing material to the size of the paper pattern. Cut out the purple silk, placing the pattern on the bias and adding a 1.5 cm/⅝ in turning allowance all round.

2 Using tailor's chalk, lightly mark out freehand a swirly design on the silk piece. Remember to match up the pattern at the two ends of the fabric. Random curlicues are shown here, but you could substitute a pattern of your choice.

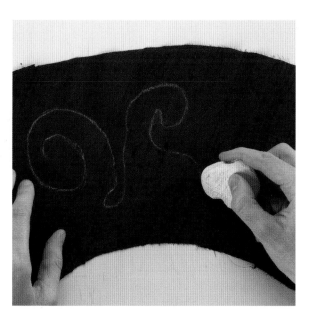

3 Lay the cord along the marked line. Thread a needle with matching thread and make small stitches over the cord, couching it to the silk.

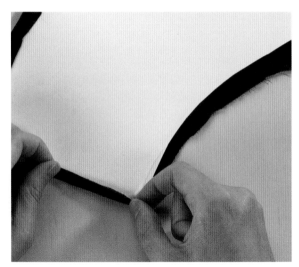

4 Lay the fabric face down. Remove the paper from the backing material and position it centrally on the silk. Smooth out the fabric from the middle outwards. Apply a line of glue all round the edges of the backing material. Fold the turning allowance to the wrong side and press down.

5 Wrap the frame with binding tape (see Techniques). Apply glue to the outside of the rings and the upright struts. Wrap the backed fabric around the frame. Apply a line of glue to the underside of the overlap and stick to the inner edge of the shade. Use two clothes pegs (pins) to hold the edges together until the glue is dry. Slip-stitch the folded edges in place. Spray the shade with flame retarder if necessary before fitting the shade on to the lamp base.

SEQUINNED ORGANZA SHADE

*Extravagantly decorated with vibrant metal-shot organza, sequins and a sparkling
fringe, this shimmering design is influenced by Indian tinsel ornaments and will look
wonderful in a setting of strong, bright colours.*

YOU WILL NEED
paper
pencil
ready-made empire lampshade
scissors
0.5 m/½ yd orange metallic organza
spray adhesive and face mask
PVA (white) glue
scraps of organza in different colours
fine needle
multicoloured large sequins
small glass beads
matching thread
metallic fringe
household sponge
enamel paint in dark orange and gold
wooden lamp base
paintbrush

1 Make a paper pattern to fit the frame (see
Techniques). Cut two pieces of metallic-coloured
organza, placing the pattern on the bias and adding
2.5 cm/1 in all round. Wearing a protective face
mask, lightly coat the shade with spray adhesive.
Wrap one piece of organza around the shade, turn
under 1.5 cm/⅝ in on one side edge, apply a line of
PVA (white) glue to the inside and lap (press) it over
the opposite raw edge. Repeat this process with the
second piece of fabric.

2 Apply a thin line of PVA (white) glue around
the inside of the top edge of each piece of fabric
and fold over the excess fabric. At the bottom, trim
the fabric level with the edge for a neat finish.

▶

3 Cut some 4 cm/1½ in squares of organza in bright, contrasting colours. To fray the fabric, use a fine needle to separate and remove threads from the edges of the squares then fray gently with your fingers.

4 Assemble pairs of squares in contrasting colours and stitch through with a sequin and some small glass beads to the centre of each pair. Make each decoration unique using different colours and shapes of beads and sequins.

5 Glue a decorative square into place on the shade, using a small blob of PVA (white) glue, avoiding the fringed edges. Position the rest of the decorations at random over the shade and leave to dry completely.

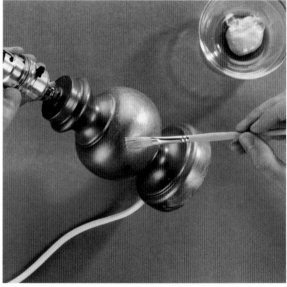

6 Cut a length of metallic fringe to fit around the bottom edge of the frame, plus a 2 cm/¾ in overlap. Apply a line of glue around the bottom edge and press the fringe in place around the shade. Turn in 1 cm/½ in at one end of the fringe, lap it over the opposite raw edge and stick in position.

7 Using a piece of household sponge, apply a coat of orange paint to the lamp base. Leave to dry, then apply a thin coat of gold paint using a paintbrush allowing the orange to show through. Leave to dry. Spray the shade with flame retarder if necessary, before fixing the shade. Use a low-wattage bulb.

PAPER CIRCLES AND BUTTONS

This is a really quick and easy way to turn a plain ready-made lampshade into a striking decorative feature. These papers have been chosen to go well with a wooden base, but you could match any existing colour scheme this way.

YOU WILL NEED
handmade paper in black and brown
pencil
paper glue
ready-made cone-shaped lampshade
12 mother-of-pearl buttons
needle
matching thread
wooden lamp base

1 Draw 12 circles on black paper and 12 on brown, approximately 3 cm/1¼ in in diameter. Draw another 12 circles on each paper approximately 2 cm/ ¾ in in diameter. Tear out the circles following the pencil lines.

2 Glue the larger circles all over the shade with a small blob of paper glue, spacing them evenly. Stick the smaller circles in the centre of the larger ones, gluing the brown to the black paper and vice versa.

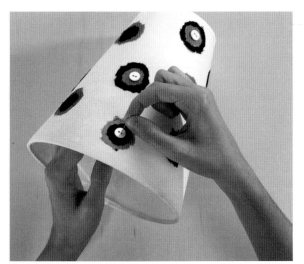

3 When the glue is dry, position a button at the centre of each paper circle and stitch in place.

4 Spray the shade with flame retarder before attaching the shade to a wooden lamp base.

SATIN AND VELVET RIBBON DRUM

The cover for this lampshade consists entirely of ribbons, allowing you to introduce a rich variety of colour and texture. The ribbons are simply stuck side by side on to a piece of lampshade backing material to create the striped effect.

YOU WILL NEED
paper
pencil
drum-shaped lampshade frame with reversible gimbal, top diameter 18 cm/7 in, bottom diameter 20 cm/8 in, height 20 cm/8 in
scissors
self-adhesive lampshade backing material
satin bias binding (tape)
selection of coloured velvet and satin ribbons
all-purpose glue
clothes pegs (pins)
needle
matching thread
ceramic lamp base
spray enamel paint and face mask

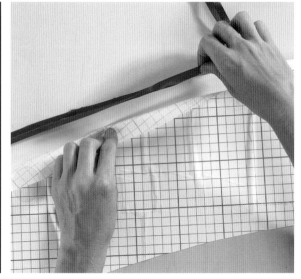

1 Make a paper pattern to fit the frame (see Techniques). Cut a piece of self-adhesive backing material to the size of the paper pattern. Remove the backing paper from the lower edge of the backing material to expose the adhesive. Cut a piece of satin bias binding (tape) to the length of the lower edge plus 2 cm/¾ in. Press one edge of the bias binding to the lower edge of the backing material.

2 Cut lengths of satin and velvet ribbon to the length of the circumference of your shade leaving a 1 cm/½ in overlap at one end. Lay a length of ribbon alongside the bias binding, following the curve of the pattern. Lay more lengths of ribbon across the backing material until the last one is 5 mm/¼ in from the top edge. Build up the pattern, alternating velvet with satin of different colours, gradually removing the backing paper as you work.

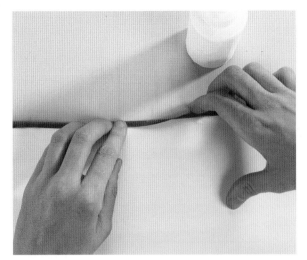

3 Cut a piece of satin bias binding to the length of the top edge, adding a 2 cm/¾ in turning allowance. Lay one edge of the bias binding along the top edge. Apply a line of glue to the wrong side of the backing material at the top and bottom edges. Fold the binding over to the wrong side.

4 Apply a thin line of glue to the side edge and fold the raw ribbon ends to the wrong side. Leave to dry. If the ribbons begin to curl away from the backing material, place under a heavy object such as a book to flatten until dry. Neaten any untidy edges or hanging threads with scissors.

5 Apply a thin line of glue to the underside of the same edge. Take care to wipe away any glue which squeezes on to the ribbons. Roll into a drum and lap (press) the glued edge over the opposite edge, matching up the stripes of colours perfectly. Use two clothes pegs (pins) to hold the edges together firmly at the top and bottom until the glue is completely dry.

6 Where the raw edges of the bias binding meet, turn under 1 cm/½ in of one raw edge and stick it down so that it overlaps the other raw edge. Use the clothes pegs (pins) to hold the bindings together until the glue is dry. Slip-stitch the folded edge in place. Apply a line of glue to the outside edge of the frame and insert it into the cover.

7 Working in a well-ventilated space, and wearing a face mask, spray the lamp base with a thin coat of pink enamel paint. Leave to dry before applying a second coat. Spray the shade with flame retarder if necessary, before attaching to the base. Use a medium-wattage bulb.

CUTWORK LAMPSHADE

*Light and shadows play around the delicate sculpted pattern circling the bottom of this pendant
shade, both in daylight and when lit from within. The pure white parchment is sprayed gold
inside, to give extra sparkle to the light.*

YOU WILL NEED

paper
pencil
scissors
A1 (594 x 841 mm/23⅜ x 33⅛ in) sheet of
parchment paper
gold spray paint and face mask
ruler
tracing paper
card for template
cutting mat
craft knife
eraser
PVA (white) glue
clothes pegs (pins)
20 cm/8 in diameter plain ring
masking tape
glue gun
15 cm/6 in diameter flush pendant ring

1 Make a paper pattern (see Techniques). The length of the upper arc should be 50 cm/19¾ in; the length of the lower arc should be 65 cm/25¾ in (including overlap) and the height 35 cm/13¾ in. Draw a wavy line freehand along one side edge with a pencil and cut the pattern out.

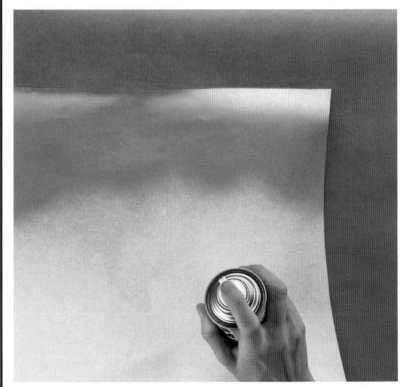

2 Transfer the pattern on to the parchment paper and cut out. In a well-ventilated space and wearing a face mask, apply an even layer of gold spray paint to one side of the paper.

60

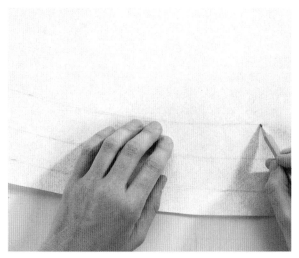

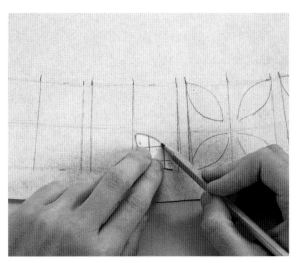

3 On the plain side, 3 cm/1¼ in from the bottom edge, mark three parallel lines 3 cm/1¼ in apart. Draw vertical lines at 6 cm/2¼ in and 1 cm/½ in intervals alternately, to make "boxes", adjusting the boxes to fit along the curved lines. Then mark vertical lines dividing the boxes in half.

4 Trace the petal pattern from the back of the book and make a template from thin card. Position one point of the petal at one corner of the box and the other point at the centre. Draw around the petal using a pencil. Repeat for all corners to give a four-petalled flower. Mark all the flowers.

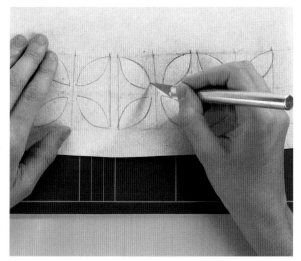

5 Lay the parchment paper on a cutting mat. Using a craft knife, carefully cut along one side of the petal from point to point. On the other side, cut 4 mm/⅛ in from one point to 4 mm/⅛ in from the other point, so that the centre of the petal is joined by two tabs.

6 Remove the pencil lines with an eraser. Using a ruler and the blunt edge of a pair of scissors, score a line from top point to bottom point on each petal. Carefully fold along the scored lines so that each petal stands out in relief.

▶

7 Apply a line of glue along the right side of the straight side edge. Roll the shade into a cone shape and lap the wavy edge over the straight side edge. Use two clothes pegs (pins) to hold the edges firmly until the glue is dry. Fit the plain ring just inside the bottom edge of the shade. Hold it in place temporarily with strips of masking tape.

8 Use a glue gun to apply evenly spaced blobs of PVA (white) glue to the outside of the ring. Roll the paper edge over the ring to cover it. Use clothes pegs (pins) to hold the edge firmly in place until the glue is dry. Fit and glue the flush pendant ring at the top in the same way. Spray the shade with flame retarder if necessary and attach to the pendant fitting.

WOVEN RIBBON SCONCE

Silk ribbon is available in stunning, lustrous colours and makes an original woven shade for this sconce. Use wired ribbon to keep the lines straight and the corners of the square shade crisp. Narrower ribbon in a matching shade is used to bind the edges.

YOU WILL NEED
square lampshade frame with bulb clip, top 9 cm/3½ in, bottom
12.5 cm/5 in, height 10 cm/4 in
binding tape
scissors
2.2 m/2½ yd each wired silk ribbon in two colours, 2.5 cm/1 in wide
pins
needle
matching thread
1.5 m/1½ yd wired silk ribbon, 1.5 cm/⅝ in wide in a
matching colour
brass single wall sconce
gold spray enamel paint and face mask

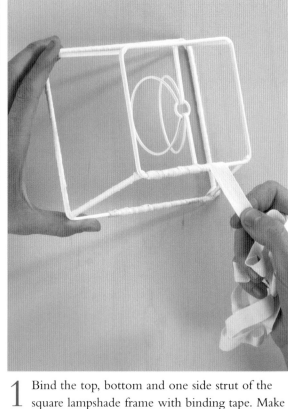

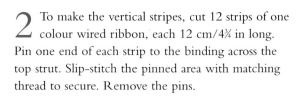

1 Bind the top, bottom and one side strut of the square lampshade frame with binding tape. Make sure you cover the struts completely.

2 To make the vertical stripes, cut 12 strips of one colour wired ribbon, each 12 cm/4¾ in long. Pin one end of each strip to the binding across the top strut. Slip-stitch the pinned area with matching thread to secure. Remove the pins.

3 Pull the ribbons taut and pin and slip-stitch the other ends to the binding tape on the bottom strut. Try to keep the ribbons close together with a small gap in between. Continue steps 2 and 3 all around the frame until covered with vertical stripes.

4 For the horizontal stripes, cut four lengths of contrasting ribbon 51 cm/20 in long. Working from the top to the bottom, pin each length to the bound side strut, spreading them out evenly. Slip-stitch the horizontal ribbons in position at one end.

5 Starting from the top, weave the horizontal ribbons in and out of the vertical ones all round the shade. Pin the ends to the bound side strut and trim to leave a 1 cm/½ in turning allowance.

6 Turn the seam allowances under and lap (press) them over the opposite raw edges. Slip-stitch the ribbons into place.

7 To conceal the ribbon ends, cut two lengths of narrower 1.5 cm/⅝ in ribbon to fit the top and bottom edges, adding a 2.5 cm/1 in turning allowance. Fold the ribbon over the strut lengthways and secure both edges with widely spaced slip stitch. Turn under 1.5 cm/⅝ in at the end, lap it over the opposite end and slip-stitch.

8 In a well-ventilated room, and wearing a face mask, spray the brass wall sconce with a coat of gold enamel spray paint. Leave to dry completely. Spray the shade with flame retarder if necessary before attaching the shade to the sconce.

TWO-WAY PLEATS

This taffeta shade has been given a smart, ribbed surface with narrow machine-stitched pleats running in both directions. Alternating the direction of stitching for the horizontal pleats produces a wavy effect in the vertical lines.

YOU WILL NEED
paper
pencil
drum frame with reversible gimbal fitting, top diameter 20 cm/8 in, bottom diameter 25 cm/10 in, height 25 cm/10 in
binding tape
140 x 50 cm/55 x 20 in blue taffeta
iron
sewing machine
matching thread
scissors
self-adhesive backing material
PVA (white) glue
satin bias binding (tape)
clothes pegs (pins)
needle
wooden lamp base
sandpaper
cloth (clean cotton rag)
finishing wax

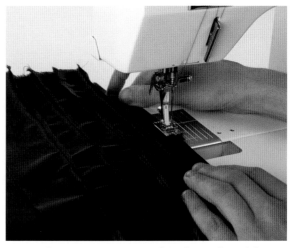

1 Make a paper pattern to fit a drum-shaped frame (see Techniques). Wrap all the struts of the frame with binding tape until completely covered (see Techniques). Press in pleats 2.5 cm/1 in apart across the width of the fabric. Machine-stitch each pleat 5 mm/¼ in from the folded edge.

2 Press in pleats at right angles to the first, 6 cm/2½ in apart. Machine-stitch 5 mm/¼ in from the fold lines. ▶

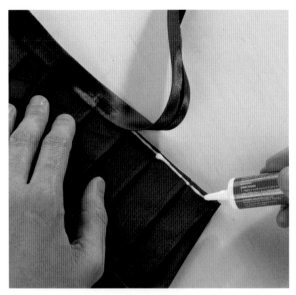

3 Cut a piece of backing material to the size of the paper pattern. Cut out the pleated taffeta to the same pattern, adding a 1.5 cm/⅝ in seam allowance all around. Lay the taffeta face down, peel away the paper from the backing material, and position it centrally. Smooth out the fabric from the middle outwards. Apply a line of glue all round the edges of the backing material and turn in the allowance. Cut a length of satin bias binding (tape) to fit the bottom, adding a 2 cm/¾ in overlap. Apply a line of glue along the bottom of the taffeta and lay one edge of the bias binding along it.

4 Apply glue to the outside of the rings and the upright struts. Wrap the backed fabric around the frame. Squeeze a line of glue along the underside of the overlap and stick to the inner edge of the shade. Use two clothes pegs (pins) to hold the edges together firmly until the glue is dry. Squeeze a line of glue around the underside of the bottom edge and fold the binding over. Where the ends of the binding meet, turn under 1 cm/½ in at one end and stick it down so that it overlaps the other raw end. Use a clothes peg (pin) to hold it firmly until the glue is dry. Slip-stitch the folded edges to secure.

5 Lightly rub the lamp base with sandpaper then, using a cloth, rub over the finishing wax. Spray the shade with flame retarder if necessary and attach to the base. Fit with a low-wattage bulb.

RIBBON ROSETTES

Crisp black-and-white gingham ribbons folded into simple, precise bows give this smart cream shade a sophisticated finish that is a world away from the country-style ruffles usually associated with this traditional patterned fabric.

YOU WILL NEED
tape measure
ready-made drum-shaped lampshade
paper
pencil
scissors
openweave linen
spray adhesive and face mask
PVA (white) glue
for each large rosette: gingham ribbon, 2 cm/¾ in wide
for each medium rosette: gingham ribbon, 15 mm/⅝ in wide
for each small rosette: gingham ribbon, 8 mm/⅜ in wide, plus
2 m/2 yd for trimming
needle
matching thread
buttons
wooden pillar lamp base
paintbrush
matt black acrylic paint

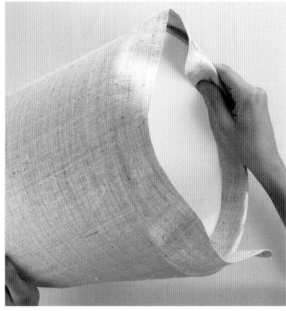

1 Measure the length and circumference of the shade and make a paper pattern (see Techniques). Cut a piece of linen to the size of the pattern, adding a 2 cm/¾ in turning allowance all round. Wearing a face mask, spray the shade lightly with a coat of spray adhesive. Wrap the linen around the shade, turn under 1 cm/½ in along one side edge, apply a line of glue to the inside and lap (press) it over the opposite edge. Squeeze a line of glue around the inside of the top and bottom edges of the shade and fold the excess fabric over.

2 For each ribbon rosette, lightly fold the length of ribbon into six parts. Starting at one end, use the fold lines as a guide to create six petals around a central point. Make a small stitch to secure each one in place at the centre.

3 Position a small button in the centre of each rosette and stitch in place.

4 Arrange the rosettes in a random but even pattern over the shade and glue in place.

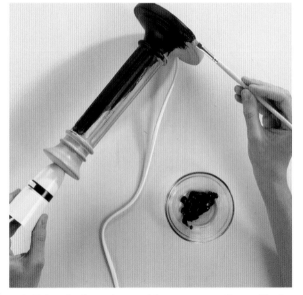

5 Cut two lengths of narrow ribbon to fit the top and bottom edges plus 2 cm/¾ in. Apply a line of glue around the bottom edge and press the ribbon in place around the shade. Turn under 1 cm/½ in at one end of the ribbon, lap it over the opposite raw edge and stick in place. Repeat for the top edge.

6 Paint the lamp base with two coats of matt black acrylic paint, allowing the paint to dry thoroughly between applications and avoiding the fittings and wire. Spray the shade with flame retarder if necessary, and leave to dry before attaching the shade to the base. Fit with a low-wattage bulb.

PLEATED SATIN SCONCE

A single or double sconce, elegantly yet simply dressed in glimmering pleated satin, will look perfectly at home in the grandest of rooms. Pick a rich, deep colour that will complement the wall behind it and shed a warm, flattering light.

YOU WILL NEED

paper
half wall sconce lampshade frame with bulb clip, top diameter
8 cm/3¼ in, bottom diameter 13 cm/5 in, height 12 cm/4¾ in
pencil
scissors
binding tape
0.5 m/½ yd gold satin
ruler
tailor's chalk
iron
sewing machine
matching thread
self-adhesive lampshade backing material
PVA (white) glue
brown satin bias binding (tape)
tape measure
clothes pegs (pins)
brass wall sconce

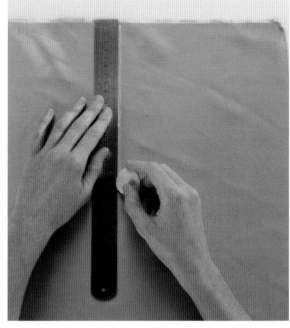

1 Make a paper pattern to fit the sconce frame. Lay out a sheet of paper and place the frame on its side at one corner. Draw along one upright strut, roll the frame across the sheet in an arc, marking the outside of the top and bottom struts, until the opposite strut touches the paper. Draw along the outside edge of this strut. Cut out the pattern and check its fit over the frame. Wrap the frame with binding tape. Along the length of the fabric mark and press in pleats 2 cm/¾ in apart.

2 Machine-stitch the pleats 5 mm/¼ in from the fold lines. Place the paper pattern on the pleated fabric so that the pleats run horizontally across the middle of the shade, and cut out the fabric, adding 1.5 cm/⅝ in all round. ▶

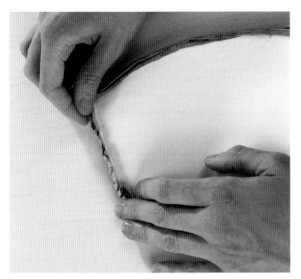

3 Cut the backing material to the size of the paper pattern. Lay the satin face down. Peel away the backing paper and place the backing material centrally on the fabric. Smooth out the fabric from the middle outwards. Apply a line of glue all round the edges of the backing material and turn in the allowance.

4 Cut two lengths of bias binding (tape) to fit the top and bottom of the shade, adding a 2 cm/¾ in turning allowance. Turn under 1 cm/½ in at each raw end and, using PVA (white) glue, stick the binding in position along the edges of the satin, folding the binding over the turned-in ends for a neat finish.

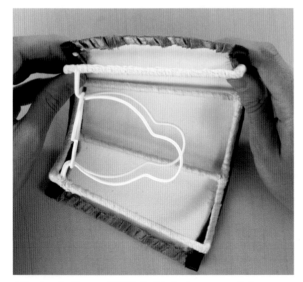

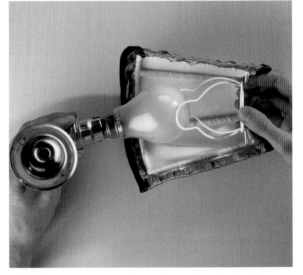

5 Apply lines of PVA (white) glue around the outside edges of the frame and position the shade over it. Use clothes pegs (pins) to hold the shade firmly in place until the glue is dry.

6 Neaten any stray edges. Spray the shade with flame retarder if necessary, and leave to dry. Fix the finished shade to the brass wall sconce and fit with a low-wattage bulb.

SILK STRIPES

A gathered silk "skirt" is easy to sew and will make a dramatic and colourful statement, whether you buy a new, plain shade or use it to rejuvenate an existing one. The stripes could be of uniform or random widths, as you prefer.

YOU WILL NEED
tape measure
ready-made Oriental lampshade
scissors
0.5 m/½ yd each lime green, magenta and
orange silk dupion
pins
sewing machine
iron
needle
matching thread
PVA (white) glue
black bobble fringing to fit top and bottom edges
wooden lamp base
fine-grade sandpaper
lime green acrylic paint
paintbrush
matt varnish

1 Measure the circumference of the bottom edge and the sloping side of the lampshade. Cut strips of each fabric of varying widths and to the length of the side plus 4 cm/1½ in. Cut enough strips to cover the bottom circumference plus a total of 6 cm/2½ in for seam allowances. Pin and machine-stitch the pieces together by their long sides, leaving 6 mm/¼ in seam allowances. Press the seams open.

2 Fold the cover right sides together and machine-stitch the short edges. Press the seam open. Press a 2 cm/¾ in hem along the top and bottom edges. Tack (baste) and machine-stitch a narrow hem along the bottom edge. To gather the top, thread a needle, double up the thread and knot the ends. Work an even running stitch all round the top edge of the shade.

▶

3 Apply a thin line of PVA (white) glue around the inside bottom edge of the shade and fold and press the bottom edge of the cover in place. Along the top edge, draw up the gathering thread, wind the thread around a pin and even out the gathers. Glue the cover to the top edge of the shade.

4 Cut a length of bobble fringing to fit the bottom edge of the shade, adding a 2 cm/¾ in turning allowance. Slip-stitch the fringing in place. Turn under 1 cm/½ in at one end of the fringing and lap (press) it over the opposite raw edge. Stitch in position. Repeat at the top of the shade.

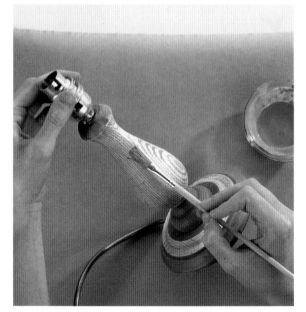

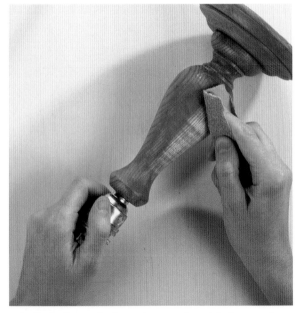

5 Rub down the lamp base using fine-grade sandpaper to remove any varnish. Paint with a coat of thinned lime green paint and leave to dry.

6 Rub down the lamp base again with fine-grade sandpaper to remove the excess paint. Seal with a coat of matt varnish.

PUNCHED PAPER SHADE

The subtle punched decorations on this parchment shade will come to life when the lamp is lit.
This shade draws inspiration from the punched designs worked on sheets of metal to make the
"dark lanterns" of the seventeenth century.

YOU WILL NEED

paper

pencil

A3 (297 x 420 mm/11¾ x 16½ in) sheet parchment paper

scissors

pinking shears

pair of compasses (compass)

cork tile or board

bradawl

eraser

8.5 cm/3½ in diameter ring with reversible gimbal fitting

22 cm/8¾ in diameter plain ring

3 brass paper fasteners

masking tape

glue gun

metal lampstand

blue spray enamel paint and face mask

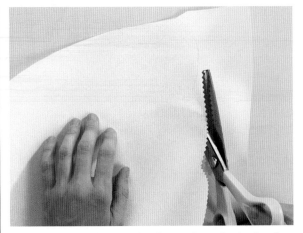

1 Scale up and copy the design from the back of the book to make a paper template. Trace the outline of the shade on to the parchment and cut out, cutting along the scalloped edge with pinking shears.

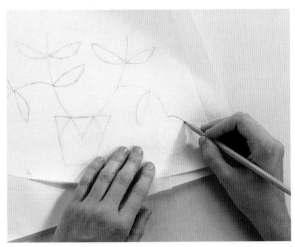

2 Lay the parchment over the template and trace the flower design with a soft pencil. Mark the circles using a pair of compasses (compass).

3 Using a cork tile or board to protect the work surface, insert the point of a bradawl at each marked point, pushing it through the parchment and twisting to make a perfectly round hole. To make a small hole insert only the point; for larger holes, push the spike in further and twist. Make a large hole in each scallop along the side. Rub out the pencil marks.

4 Roll the parchment into a cone shape and slip it over the rings to check the fit. Lap (press) the scalloped edge over the straight edge and mark the positions of the three holes in the scallops on the underlap. Punch the three holes with the bradawl. These will form the eyelets to fasten the shade around the rings.

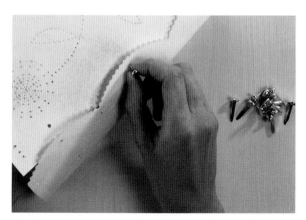

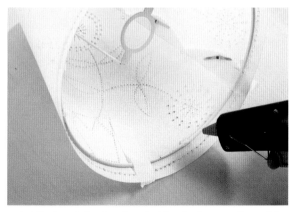

5 Push a brass paper fastener through each hole to fasten the edges together, with domed head of the fastener on the scalloped overlap. Open the shanks of the fasteners on the inside of the shade.

6 Fit the plain ring just inside the lower edge of the shade and hold in place with masking tape. Use a glue gun to apply evenly spaced blobs of glue to the ring. Fit and glue the upper ring in the same way.

▶

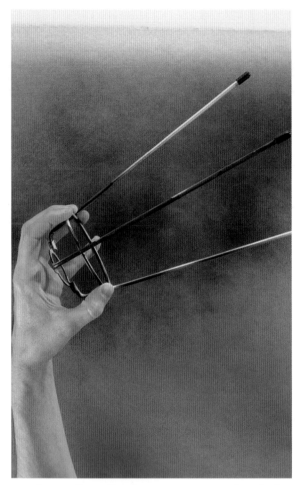

7 In a well-ventilated space, on a protective plastic
or paper surface and, wearing a face mask, spray
the metal lampstand with an even coat of blue enamel
paint. Leave to dry before applying a second coat.
Spray the shade with flame retarder if necessary, and
leave to dry before assembling the lamp.

MATERIALS

Basic materials for making lampshades and decorating lamp bases can be purchased from haberdashers (notions stores) or craft suppliers. Specialist materials are available by mail order.

BEADING WIRE
This is available plated in gold or silver in many sizes to fit beads.

BINDINGS
Binding tape is a specialist 1 cm/ ½ in wide bias tape for binding lampshade frames. Bias binding (tape), used to cover raw edges, is a narrow strip of cotton, satin or other fabric, cut on the cross.

FABRIC
Select a fabric that will give a good light. White or light coloured fabrics will shed the most light. Lightweight silk and cotton are the best and easiest fabrics to use. Fabric lampshades should always be rendered fireproof with a flame retarder spray before use (see Techniques).

GLUE
Use a strong all-purpose household glue to join lampshade covers and glue in the frames. Spray adhesive can be used to attach a fabric cover. Good ventilation is essential when using spray glue and you may wish to use a protective face mask.

GOLD LEAF AND WAX GILT
Dutch gold leaf is an alternative to gold leaf. Picture framer's wax gilt can be rubbed on to lamp bases using a cloth (rag) or your finger for a soft gold sheen.

PAINTS
Acrylic paints are quick-drying, water-based paints that give a hard finish. Enamel spray paint gives an even coat to a variety of surfaces, including wood and metal. Protect the work area with newspaper and ensure the room is well ventilated. Always wear gloves and a mask.

PAPER
Handmade paper and artificial parchment are ideal for shades. Handmade tissue is useful for lining paper shades.

RIBBON
Ribbons can be used to cover shades made of self-adhesive backing material. They can also be woven around frames without backing, and used for trimming.

RINGS
Rings differ from frames as they have no vertical struts. They should be used for paper shades to avoid the struts showing through when the light is switched on. Purchase one ring, to fit either the top or bottom of the shade, with a flush pendant or reversible gimbal fitting, and one plain ring to fit the other end.

SELF-ADHESIVE BACKING MATERIAL
Available from specialist craft suppliers, this gives stiffness and body to fabric lampshades.

THREAD
Use 100% cotton or a polyester blend of thread. Select a thread a shade darker than the fabric you are sewing.

TRIMMINGS
A wide range of trimmings such as ric-rac braid, tassels, bobbles and fringing is available for decorating the edges of shades. Many other materials can be glued or stitched into place, including sequins, glass beads and buttons. Artificial silk and velvet shaped flowers can be cut from their stems and glued to the shade. Pompoms can be handmade from spun cotton knitting yarn.

Opposite, clockwise from left: frames; masking tape; raffia; trimmings; glues; Dutch gold leaf; acrylic, enamel and spray paints; paper; self-adhesive backing material; beading wire; pompom; threads; paper fasteners; buttons and beads.

EQUIPMENT

You will probably already have most of the equipment required to make lampshades and decorate lamp bases. Everything can be purchased from haberdashers (notions stores) or craft suppliers.

BRADAWL
A tool with a long steel point used to make holes in paper or card.

CLOTHES PEGS (PINS)
Use these to hold glued overlapped edges together firmly while the glue is drying.

CRAFT KNIFE
Used to cut card and paper. Always cut away from your body, and protect the work surface with a mat or board. Use the back of the knife blade to score fold lines.

CUTTING MAT AND CORK BOARD
A rubber non-slip surface protects the work surface when you are cutting. Use a cork tile or board to protect the work surface when using a bradawl to punch holes.

GLUE GUN
This specialized tool heats up pellets of solid glue until they are liquid and translucent. The glue is strong and dries almost instantly.

HOLE PUNCH
Use a standard office punch to make holes in paper and card.

IRON
Use an iron to press seams open or pleats flat and to flatten fabric.

JEWELLERY PLIERS AND CUTTERS
Use these for bending and cutting beading wire.

NEEDLES
Keep a good selection of sizes for hand-sewing. Use needles with a large eye for embroidery threads (floss) or yarn. A specialized beading needle is fine enough to fit through the centre holes of the smallest beads.

PAINTBRUSHES
Use a narrow decorating brush, or an artist's brush for finer work. Buy good quality brushes, as cheaper ones are more likely to shed hairs and loose definition. An ordinary sponge can also be used to apply paint to give interesting surface effects.

PENCILS AND CHALKS
A soft pencil should be used to mark designs on paper shades, so that the marks can be easily erased. A dressmaker's pencil or tailor's chalk can be used for marking fabric and brushed off later.

PINS
Use ordinary dressmaking pins to hold fabrics in place temporarily: discard any blunt or rusty pins which may mark the fabric.

RULER AND TAPE MEASURE
Use a metal ruler as a straight edge when cutting with a craft knife. A metal or plastic ruler is needed for marking fabric, drawing templates or measuring straight edges. Use a dressmaker's tape measure to measure curved edges.

SCISSORS
Always use separate scissors for cutting paper and fabrics, as paper will blunt the blades. Embroidery scissors are useful for cutting threads and smaller pieces of fabric. Pinking shears have serrated blades which are useful for neatening raw edges and can also be used for decorative effects.

SET SQUARE (T SQUARE)
Used to draft accurate right angles.

SEWING MACHINE
A basic sewing machine with straight stitch and zig-zag stitches is invaluable.

Opposite, clockwise from left: cutting mat; craft knife; set square (T square); sewing machine; glue gun; tape measure; ruler; pencil; paintbrush; clothes pegs (pins); tailor's chalk; pins; needles; iron; hole punches; pliers; embroidery and paper scissors; pinking shears; cork board; bradawl.

TECHNIQUES

Making and decorating lampshades and bases is simple to do, and once you have mastered a few simple techniques you will be able to create a variety of exciting lamps.

MAKING BIAS BINDING (TAPE)

Bias binding strips may be used to wrap frames, cover raw edges or to bind edges decoratively.

1 Cut a rectangular piece of fabric on the straight grain. Fold down one top corner to meet the bottom edge, forming a diagonal fold. Press.

2 Open out the fabric. Mark parallel lines diagonally across the fabric 3 cm/1¼ in apart and cut out the strips.

GATHERING FABRIC

3 Pin the short edges together as shown and stitch the seam, using a sewing machine. Press the seam allowance open.

Thread a needle, double up the thread and tie a knot in the ends. Work an even running stitch the length of the fabric, draw up the thread, wind it around a pin and even out the gathers.

BINDING A FRAME USING BIAS BINDING OR BINDING TAPE

Bind the frame to ensure a good surface for gluing a fabric cover or to stitch fabric to a frame.

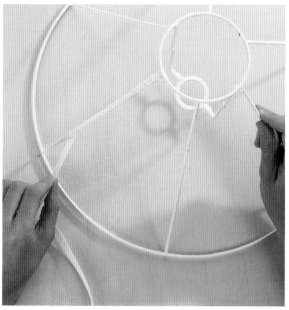

To start winding, turn 2.5 cm/1 in of the tape over a strut and wind the tape along the strut at a 45° angle. Secure the end with a few small stitches.

MEASURING A CONE-SHAPED FRAME

1 To find the circumference of the top and bottom of a cone-shaped frame, measure the diameter and multiply by three.

MAKING A PAPER PATTERN FOR A CONE-SHAPED OR DRUM FRAME

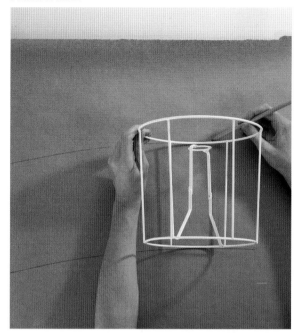

Place the frame at the end of a piece of paper. Draw along one upright strut, then roll the frame across the paper in an arc, marking the course of the outside top and bottom rings until the first strut touches the paper again. Add a 1 cm/½ in overlap allowance on one side. Cut out and check it fits the frame.

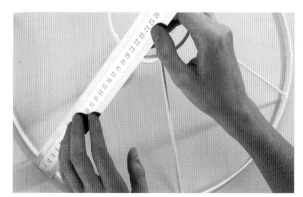

2 To find the height of a cone-shaped frame, measure the angled side of the frame, including the struts.

MEASURING FOR A SHADE USING TWO RINGS

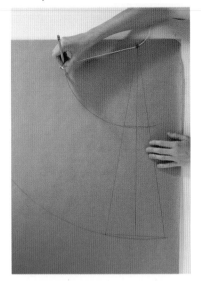

MAKING A LAMPSHADE USING
SELF-ADHESIVE BACKING MATERIAL
Lampshades can be simple to make
and homemade versions will fit
your own requirements perfectly.

1 Measure the diameter of the
top and bottom rings. In the
corner of a sheet of paper, parallel
to the bottom, mark the diameter
of the bottom ring. Draw a
vertical line at right angles,
bisecting the first line. Mark a
point along the vertical line the
desired height of the shade. At this
point draw a horizontal line the
length of the diameter of the top
ring. The mid-point should
intersect the vertical line. Draw a
diagonal line from the end of the
bottom line to the end of the top
line, and continue until it meets
the vertical line. Repeat on the
other side. Attach a pencil to a
piece of string, and place the
pencil on one of the points where
the top horizontal line meets the
diagonal. Pin the string at the
point where the vertical and
diagonal lines intersect. Draw an
arc. Repeat, using the bottom line.

2 Calculate the length of the
circumference of the top ring
and mark this measurement on the
upper arc, starting from one of the
diagonal lines. Mark the length of
the circumference of the bottom
ring on the lower arc. Join these
two points. Add a 1 cm/½ in
overlap allowance to the side edge.

FLAMEPROOFING A LAMPSHADE
Fabric and paper must be rendered
flameproof. Before use, all shades
and decorations should be sprayed
with flame retardant spray. Spray
in a well-ventilated area, wearing
a protective face mask if you suffer
from any respiratory problems.
Protective rubber (latex) gloves
are also advised. For application,
follow the manufacturer's
instructions. Always ensure that
both the shade and frame are dry
before attaching any wires or
exposing them to electricity.

1 Cut out the backing material
to the size of the lampshade
template. For the lampshade cover,
lay the template on the fabric on
the cross. Draw around it, adding
a turning allowance of 1.5 cm/
⅝ in all round, and cut out.
Remove the backing paper from
the backing material and place it
sticky side down on the wrong
side of the fabric, leaving an even
turning allowance all round the
backing material. Smooth out the
fabric from the middle outwards.

2 Clip away the corners 5 mm/ ¼ in from the corners of the backing material. Apply a line of glue around the turning allowance and fold it in half.

3 Apply another thin line of glue around the turning allowance, fold over all four corners, and then fold in the top and side edges.

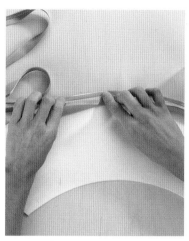

4 Apply a thin line of glue around the bottom edge. Press one side of the bias binding (tape) in position, all the way along the bottom edge.

5 Wrap the frame cover around the frame now or insert once the cover is glued and stitched. To wrap the frame, apply glue to the outside edges of the rings and struts and wrap the cover around the frame. Squeeze a line of glue along the inside of one side edge and lap (press) it over the opposite edge. Hold the edges firmly with two clothes pegs (pins) until dry.

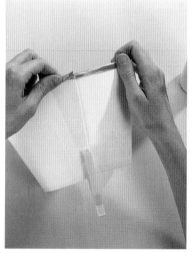

6 Where the ends of the bias binding meet, turn under 1 cm/½ in of one raw end and stick it down so that it overlaps the other raw end.

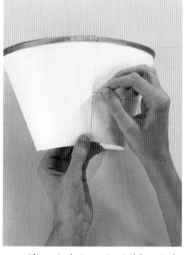

7 Slip stitch is an invisible stitch used to join folded edges and attach trimmings. With the needle, catch a thread under the fabric together with a thread on the fold of the fabric or trimming and make tiny, neat, evenly-spaced stitches.

TEMPLATES

The templates given here can be scaled up or down using a photocopier, to suit the size of your shade.

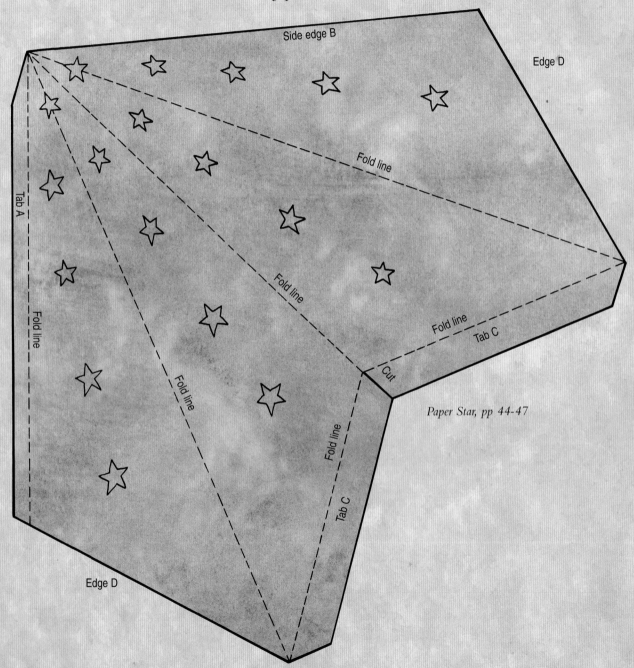

Side edge B

Edge D

Fold line

Fold line

Fold line

Tab A

Fold line

Tab C

Cut

Fold line

Tab C

Fold line

Edge D

Paper Star, pp 44-47

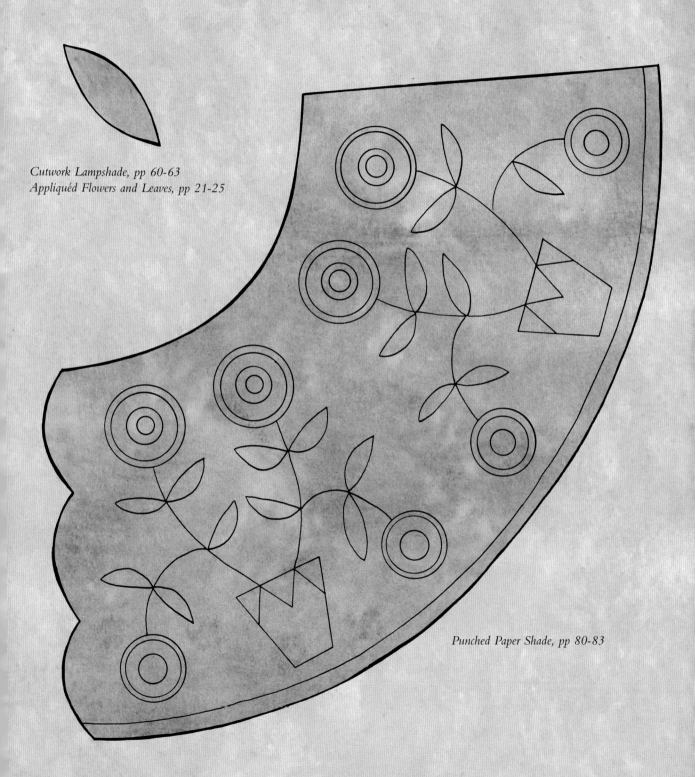

Cutwork Lampshade, pp 60-63
Appliquéd Flowers and Leaves, pp 21-25

Punched Paper Shade, pp 80-83

SHAPES OF SHADES

Lampshade frames come in many shapes and sizes: a selection from the book is shown below.
Choose a shade that covers both the bulb and the electric fitting. Various fittings are available:
a bulb clip fits on to the bulb itself and is suitable only for small, lightweight lampshades.
A reversible gimbal is used for table lamps and a pendant fitting is suitable for hanging shades.

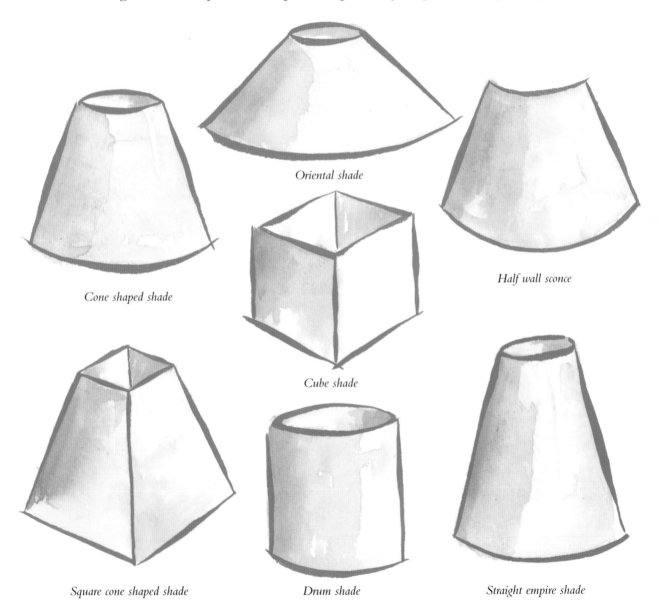

Oriental shade

Cone shaped shade

Half wall sconce

Cube shade

Square cone shaped shade

Drum shade

Straight empire shade

INDEX

ACKNOWLEDGEMENTS

The publishers would like to thank the following people for designing
projects for this book: Petra Boase for the projects on pages 26–28,
40–43; Lisa Brown for the projects on pages 29–31, 54–55, 64–67; Zoe
Clayton for the projects on pages 11–13, 18–20, 48–50, 68–70, 74–76;
Lucinda Ganderton for the projects on pages 51–53, 71–73, 77–79 and
Isabel Stanley for the projects on pages 8–10, 14–17, 21–25, 32–36,
37–39, 44–47, 56–59, 60–63, 80–83. The publishers would also like to
thank Moira Govan; C M Offray and Sons, Fir Tree Place, Church Road,
Ashford, Middlesex, TW15 2PH, England, tel: (0) 1784 247281 for
supplying the ribbon on pages 71–73.

SAFETY NOTE

The paper or fabric shade should not touch the bulb, which should be
at least 3 cm/1¼ in away from the inside of the shade to avoid a fire
hazard. Fabrics should be treated to make them flame-retardant (see
Techniques). Use a 40 watt bulb in small lampshades. The shade and
the base should be balanced carefully so that the lamp is not likely to
fall over. Do not put a wide or heavy shade on a slender base.